Games to Grow On

for Home and Church

Stan and Donna Leonard

a division of SP Publications, Inc.

Contents

ISBN: 0-88207-254-4
© 1976 by SP Publications, Inc. World rights reserved.
Printed in the United States of America

VICTOR BOOKS
A division of SP Publications, Inc.
P. O. Box 1825 ● Wheaton, Ill., 60187

Preface

Have you ever wondered how you could bring variety and freshness to your Bible teaching so that children will get really excited learning God's Word? We can all use new ideas for helping boys and girls discover and apply Bible truths. Learning games can be used profitably to supplement your curriculum. Games help make Bible truths stick to the lives of your students.

This manual is the result of interaction with Sunday School and Children's Church leaders in workshops over the past several years. Many of the games were made up and used in a variety of learning situations—at home, in Sunday School early time, Children's Church, and in weekday action groups. We've seen how they have enriched the lives of children.

Teachers have shared their own ideas that have been especially helpful for their classes. A number of these ideas are in this manual. Enthusiasm in sharing good ideas for Bible games is contagious. The Lord helps us stimulate and encourage one another. We hope this manual will do just this for you!

A Bible game that you have made yourself will fit the specific needs of your class simply because you know your children so well. Therefore, use the creativity God has given you to adapt ideas included in your curriculum and to make your own games. You'll find yourself discovering new ways to recycle your Sunday School papers, pupil's manuals, and teaching aids!

Thus—this sharing manual. We call it "sharing" because new games will continually be added as the Lord provides you and us with ideas and as we each "spur one another on toward . . . good deeds" (Heb. 10:24, NIV).

Sometimes a game will be more effective when used at home, or after a class session, rather than in presession. Maybe you prefer using it in your class period. Whatever suits you and the needs of your children best should be your way of using it.

Special tips:
1. Accumulate game resources, such as take-home papers, teaching aids, Bible pictures, and maps. You'll find a helpful list at the back of this manual on pages 47-48.
2. Take your time making the game. If it is worth making, it is worth doing well. Measure accurately, do your neat-as-possible lettering, and choose pictures that communicate effectively.
3. Don't be afraid of color and size. Eye appeal is a significant factor in learning motivation.
4. Plan for durability. If your children enjoy a game you will want to keep it for use again. Note how items can be made more child-proof by laminating the game with clear contact plastic. A little extra work now will save having to make repairs later.
5. Keep an eye open for resources—people and materials. A retired sign-maker who would be happy to help with hand lettering, a group of teens who could organize pictures for you, a display rack being replaced at the local store, an idea that pops out at you from a bulletin board at the public library—all can be enlisted in the Lord's service.

Don't Use This Manual Before You Read This Page!

Here are clues for getting the best use of the games in this manual:

1—**Age level:** This manual is designed for various age levels. Look for games most suitable for the children you are teaching. Some games can be adapted to different age levels.

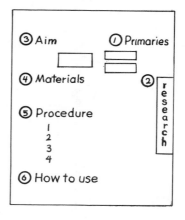

2—**Purpose:** The manual is indexed by a code word in the margin. It will help you decide how the game should be used. Sometimes a game can be used for more than one purpose. In these cases more than one code word will appear.

3—**Aim:** This brief statement will tell you how the game can best help your pupils.

4—**Materials:** Decide on the game you want to make. Take an inventory of the materials you have on hand and secure additional items needed. Assemble everything you need before you start.

5—**Procedure:** This section will tell you, step by step, how to make the game. Enjoy working on it! Don't hurry. Preparation time is invested in the lives of your children. As you work, pray that God will use this Bible learning activity to help children know Christ better.

6—**How to use:** You'll find an explanation on how the activity can be used. *When* to use it is your choice.

Plastic Pocket Tri-Folder

A Plastic Pocket Tri-Folder will be a versatile time-saver for you. A number of games in this manual have been designed exclusively for use with this Tri-Folder, and we've made a note of others which can be easily adapted for it. The more you work with your Tri-Folder the more ways you'll discover to use it.

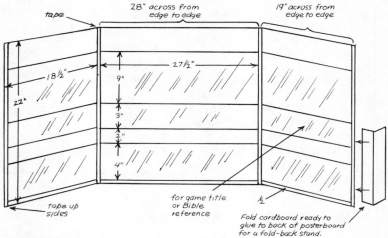

Materials:
3 sheets posterboard or illustration board, 22" x 28", all the same color
About 8 yards Mystic tape or cloth covered tape
1 yard clear plastic vinyl, medium or heavy gauge (found in fabric shops and table-covering section of department stores)
scissors, yardstick, pencil, glue

Procedure:
1. Cut 9" off two pieces of posterboard. Store these 9" pieces for future use.
2. Tape two remaining 19" pieces, one to each end of the un-cut sheet of posterboard.

6

3. Cut clear plastic into the measurements on the sketch. When completed you will have 9 pieces of clear plastic cut and ready to tape to the boards to form 9 pockets.
4. Tape *upper* level pockets so that top edge of plastic is 3″ from top of posterboard.

   Tape *middle* level pockets so that top edge of plastic is about 12½″ from top of posterboard.

   Tape *bottom* level pockets so that top of clear plastic is 4½″ from *bottom* of posterboard.

   Tape pockets up outer sides and along center folds. (The posterboards are already joined by tape. This second layer of tape will help reinforce the folds.)
5. Make a handy fold-back stand to support your Tri-Folder when you want to stand it up on a table. Cut scrap cardboard into two 12″ x 16″ pieces. Fold along the middle the long way. Glue to the back near each outer edge of the Tri-Folder.

Bible-time Occupations

r
e
s
e
a
r
c
h

r
e
c
a
l
l

Aims: Junior boys
To discover occupations of men in Bible times.
To recall Bible stories in which men had these occupations.

Materials:
Pictures from Bible Pic-
ture Dictionary Sets (see
p. 48)
2 sheets posterboard,
fiber-tip pen, 9 shoe-
strings
Hole punch, Mystic
tape, glue, scissors
Bible Picture Dictionary
(see p. 48)

put a shoestring through each hole
tape

- tax collector
- high priest
- shepherd
- potter
- King
- lawyer
- cupbearer
- scribe
- carpenter

knot

Procedure:
1. Cut out these pictures and definitions from Bible Picture
   Dictionary. Glue pictures only on a sheet of posterboard:
   tax collector, priest, king, potter, lawyer, scribe, cupbearer,
   carpenter, shepherd.
2. Hand-letter occupation titles on second sheet of posterboard.
   Glue definitions on *back* of the board.
3. Punch a hole next to each picture and title. Tie knot in one
   end of each shoestring and pull through holes next to titles.
4. Tape sheets of posterboard together.

How to use:
Have junior boys match the title of each occupation to the
appropriate picture. If they cannot, let them refer to the Bible
Picture Dictionary or to the definition on the back of the folder.
When they have made a successful match, let them name a
man from a Bible story who had the occupation. Use sponta-
neous conversation whenever possible to relate to pupils' lives.
Example: "How did God use this man to keep His people?"
(cupbearer, king); "How did God show He loved this man?"
(tax collector, shepherd); "How can God show you He loves you
today?"

8

Spin-and-Choose

Aim:
To identify Bible-time objects and to recall Bible stories in
which these objects were used.

Materials:
Pictures from your files and from Bible Picture Dictionary
Sets (see p. 48)
2 sheets posterboard, brad
3 3″ x 5″ cards, 3 small envelopes, paper clip
Scissors, rubber cement, fiber-tip pens

Procedure:
Identification folder
1. Fold one posterboard in middle and tape along fold for
   reinforcement. Cut second sheet of posterboard in half
   and tape one half to the end of full-size sheet. This will
   make a three-part folder.

2. Cut out and mount pictures on the three panels:

Clothes *(left)*	Boats *(center)*	Weapons *(right)*
robe	ark	sword
belt	ferryboat	sling
armor	grain ship	bow and arrow
mantle	Moses' basket	spear
sandals	fishing boat	chariot

3. Print captions at the top of the folder.

Optional: If you prefer to use the Plastic Pocket Tri-Folder (see p. 48) for this part of the game, mount pictures on construction paper and insert in lower pockets.

Spin board

1. Cut posterboard approximately 14″ x 16″. For a more sturdy board, glue two pieces together with rubber cement.
2. Punch hole in center of the board. From hole, draw lines to divide board into 3 sections.
3. For a spinner, insert brad through end of paper clip, then into spin board. Allow space between brad and board for clip to spin.
4. Print caption at top of board, "Spin-and-Choose."
5. Glue a small envelope to each section of the board. Label each to match the sections on the Identification Folder.
6. Cut each 3″ x 5″ card into 5 strips. On each strip print one item to match objects on the Identification Folder. For example, cards for the "clothes" envelope will match items on the left panel of the board.

How to use:

Use at home, in presession at Sunday School, or in Children's Church. Let a child spin the clip, open the appropriate envelope and choose a card. He must identify the correct item on the Identification Folder and try to name a Bible story in which the item is mentioned. If he has difficulty, he may go to completed Bible dictionary to "research" the item and discover the answer.

Can You Put These in the Right Order?

Aims: Juniors
To help juniors put Bible events in correct chronological sequence.
To help juniors recall unit stories.

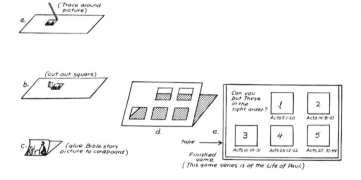

Materials:
2 pieces 18 " x 15 " cardboard or posterboard
Fiber-tip pen, rubber cement, razor blade, scissors, Mystic tape
Bible pictures, large envelope

Procedure:
1. Choose a series of stories or events from recent lessons and have on hand Bible pictures and corresponding Scripture references.
2. Trim pictures to uniform size. Then trace around each picture on one of the pieces of cardboard.

11

3. Remove pictures. Cut traced lines carefully with razor so that you leave a neat hole in cardboard for each picture.
4. Glue cardboard with holes on top of second piece of cardboard. The bottom piece will make a packing for the puzzle, so pictures will fit into the holes.
5. If necessary, cover outside edges of puzzle with tape.
6. On the top cardboard, print appropriate Scripture references to match the Bible pictures. Print numbers in the holes so that juniors will know in what order to place the pictures.
7. On the back of the puzzle, glue a large envelope for storing loose pictures when game is not in use.

How to use:
In presession have pupils look up Bible references. During or after your lesson have juniors put pictures in correct order. If time permits, have pupils retell the story of each picture.

Bible Structures

Aims: Juniors
To identify structures of Bible times.
To help children visualize settings of Bible stories.
To clarify chronological order of seven Bible events.

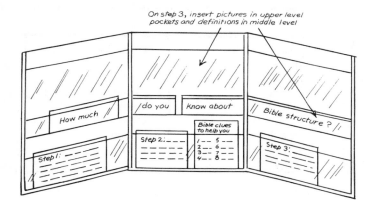

On step 3, insert pictures in upper level
pockets and definitions in middle level

Materials:
Plastic Pocket Tri-Folder (see pp. 6-7).
Pictures and definitions from Bible Picture Dictionary Sets (see p. 48).
Construction paper, scissors, fiber-tip pen

Procedure:
1. Cut out the following pictures and their definitions from the Bible Picture Dictionary Sets:
   tabernacle   palace   synagogue   theater
   Solomon's temple   city wall   courtyard
2. Mount pictures on black construction paper, trimming each picture to fit the upper-level pockets on the Tri-Folder.
3. Mount definitions on construction paper.
4. Hand-letter the game title on construction paper cards for middle-level pockets of the Tri-Folder.

13

5. Hand-letter game directions on construction paper cards to fit lower level pockets.

Step 1: Match the correct definition to each picture.

Step 2: Name one Bible fact about each structure.

Step 3: Follow clue card to arrange pictures in correct order.

Bible clues to help you:	Code for Bible clues:
1. Exodus 40:16-19	1. tabernacle
2. 1 Kings 6:11-14	2. Solomon's temple
3. Daniel 6:18	3. Babylonian palace
4. Nehemiah 2:1-4, 17-18	4. city wall
5. Matthew 4:23	5. synagogue
6. Matthew 26:69-75	6. courtyard
7. Acts 19:29-30	7. theater

front of Bible clue card   *back of Bible clue card*

How to use:
1. For Bible background research in presession.
2. In the lesson, have juniors share what they know about any structure mentioned in the Bible story.
3. For recall at the end of several units of study.

Instructions:
Insert game title in middle level pockets and game directions in lower level pockets. Display the pictures and definitions on a table and have juniors match a definition to each picture. Then have pupils follow step 2, looking in their Bibles for answers. When pupils follow step 3, have them insert pictures into top level pockets with the matching definitions beneath. (Remove game title when they put the definitions in the middle level pockets.)

Dial-n-Match

Aims: Juniors
To discover and describe Bible-time objects that will be men-
tioned in the Bible lesson.
To recall objects mentioned in past Bible stories.

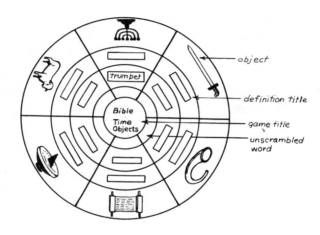

Materials:
Pictures from Bible Picture Dictionary Sets (see p. 48)
4 different colors of posterboard
fiber-tip pen, scissors, glue, brass fastener

Procedure:
1. Cut 5 circles from posterboard: 16", 10", 6½", 5", and 3"
   across (use lids to trace).
2. On largest circle find the center and punch a hole. Draw lines
   on each of the five circles to make 6 pie sections.
3. From the Bible Picture Dictionary Sets cut out objects that
   relate to current lessons. Glue one picture in each section of
   the largest circle close to the outer edge.

4. On the 10″ circle glue the definition of each object shown in the large circle but *not* in the same order as the pictures.
5. On the 6½″ circle glue the titles of the objects, using still a different order than the order on either of the larger circles.
6. On the 5″ circle print the titles scrambled.
7. On the smallest circle print the caption, Bible-time objects.
8. Punch hole in the center of each circle, assemble, and insert a brass fastener.

How to use:
Have pupils look up in presession an object from the Bible Picture Dictionary that will be in your lesson. Then have him find it on the wheel and match up the object titles and definition. He may share at the proper time in the lesson what the object looked like and give its definition. Another pupil may share an object the next week, until all objects on game circle have been used. On following Sundays, use game circle for a recall activity.

Bible Animals

Aims: **Young Juniors**

To understand how animals were used by God in Bible times.
To develop Scripture-searching skills so that pupils can begin
to find answers for themselves in the Bible.
To provide opportunity to practice Christlike manners.

1. Bible Animal Cards

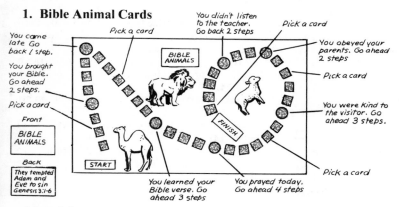

You came late Go back 1 step.

You brought your Bible. Go ahead 2 steps.

Pick a card

Front

BIBLE ANIMALS

Back

They tempted Adam and Eve to sin. Genesis 3:1-6

Pick a card

You didn't listen to the teacher. Go back 2 steps

BIBLE ANIMALS

Pick a card

You obeyed your parents. Go ahead 2 steps

Pick a card

You were kind to the visitor. Go ahead 3 steps.

Pick a card

START

You learned your Bible verse. Go ahead 3 steps

You prayed today. Go ahead 4 steps

Materials:

15 3" x 5" cards, fiber-tip pen

Procedure:

On the front of each card print the name of the game, Bible
Animals. On the back of each card print one of the numbered
statements that follow. Do not include names of animals (given
in italics). These are for your reference only.

1. The _____(serpent) tempted Adam and Eve to sin. (Gen. 3:1-6)
2. Noah sent out a _____(dove) to see if there were any dry land. (Gen. 8:8)
3. Pharaoh had a dream about seven fat _____(cows) and seven thin (cows). (Gen. 41:1-4)
4. God's people ate manna and _____(quail) when they were wandering in the wilderness. (Ex. 16:12-13)
5. David used a club to fight the _____(lions) and _____(bears) that attacked his father's sheep. (1 Sam. 17:34-35)

6. King Solomon kept beautiful _____(peacocks) in his palace. (2 Chron. 9:20-21—apes and peacocks would be acceptable)
7. The _____(ravens) brought Elijah food to eat by the Brook Cherith. (1 Kings 17:6)
8. In Bible times, _____(horses) were the symbol of military power. (Isa. 31:1)
9. Daniel was thrown into a den of wild animals. But God protected him by sending His angel to shut the _____(lions') mouths. (Dan. 6:22)
10. Jonah stayed inside a great _____(fish) for three days. (Jonah 1:17)
11. Immediately after Jesus was baptized, the Spirit of God came down from heaven in the form of a _____(dove). (Matt. 3:16)
12. Jesus said, "It is easier for a _____(camel) to go through the eye of a needle, than for a rich man to enter the king- dom of God." (Matt. 19:24)
13. The _____(donkey) carried Jesus, the Son of God, on his back. (Matt. 21:7-9)
14. The _____(sheep) heard the angels sing, "Glory to God in the highest." (Luke 2:8-14)
15. The Prodigal Son left his father's home and wound up feeding _____(swine). (Luke 15:15)

2. Game Board
Materials:
14 " x 22 " colored posterboard
30 1 " squares of various-colored construction paper
8 2 " circles of one-color construction paper
2 1 " x 3 " strips of construction paper for "start" and "finish."
Several Bible animal pictures to decorate board.

Procedure:
Glue on pictures and construction paper pieces as shown.
Neatly hand-letter instructions
on circles and squares, as
shown.

Head of brass
fastener is ⅛"
above the lid

Front
view

3. Spin Board
Materials:
Round lid from food con-
tainer, brass fastener, paper
clip

Brass fastener

Back
view

Tape over
fastener

18

Round piece of construction paper to cover lid
Fiber-tip pen, glue, scissors, tape, buttons

Procedure:
1. Using the fiber-tip pen, divide construction paper lid cover into four equal parts. Number the parts and glue on elevated side of lid.
2. Carefully poke a hole through the center of the lid.
3. Place end of paper clip over the hole.
4 Put brass fastener through paper clip and hole. Leave 1/8" space between head of fastener and lid to allow paper clip to spin.
5. Fasten and tape the back of the fastener to keep it from moving.

Instructions for playing:
Type or hand-letter the following instructions and glue to back of game board:
Ages: 6-8
Players: 2-4
Cards: Place "Bible Animals" side up.
Buttons: One for each player
Directions:
1. Each player places his button on "Start."
2. Each player spins the spin board. The player with the highest number begins the game. If two players get the same number, spin again.
3. The numbers on the spin board tell the number of moves the player can make.
4. Obey the directions given on the game board. When a player lands on "Pick a card," he must pick the top card. If he can name the missing animal, he gets another turn to spin. If he misses, he loses one turn. The card is placed at the bottom of the pile of cards. Check answers by looking up the reference in the Bible.
5. "Winner" is the first player to reach the "finish" line.

—LOUISE LOW, LOS ANGELES

19

research

From Ur to Canaan

Juniors

Aims:
To acquaint pupils with Bible lands and cities at the time of the patriarchs.
To trace Abraham's journey from Ur to Canaan.
To emphasize Abraham's tremendous faith.

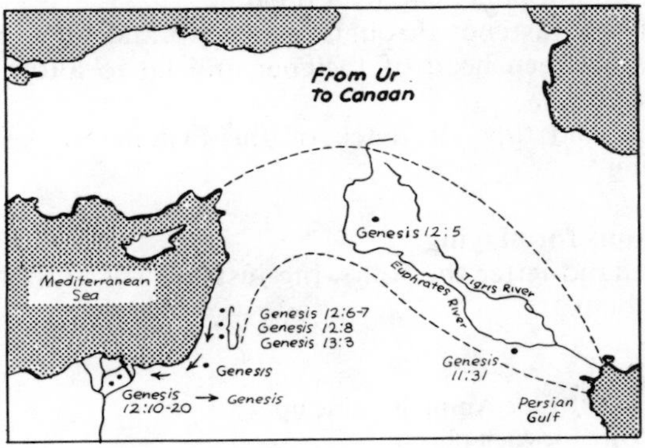

reinforce

Materials:
Map of the biblical world at the time of the patriarchs, available in the back of a Bible or in *Atlas of the Bible Lands,* No. 7-3741, $1.50. (A map for each pupil to refer to in the game would help greatly.)
Clear plastic 8″ x 11″; overhead projector
Fiber-tip pens; green and blue colored lead pencils
6 brads, 1 yard red yarn, sheet of white posterboard
2 yards clear contact plastic to laminate map

Procedure:
1. Place 8″ x 11″ plastic on a map of the biblical world at the time of patriarchs. Trace the outline of Egypt and its rivers, Canaan, the eastern edge of the Mediterranean Sea, and the Tigris and Euphrates Rivers. Put a dot on these cities: Ur, Haran, Shechem, Bethel, Beer-sheba (in the Negev), and near Tanis in Egypt.

2. Mount white posterboard on a wall and project map so that it fills posterboard.
3. Draw light lines on the posterboard. Take board down and draw over lines with black fiber-tip pen. Hand-letter captions for Mediterranean Sea, Persian Gulf, and the rivers, *but do not identify cities.*
4. Near each dot print the Bible reference in which that place is named:

Ur—Genesis 11:31
Haran—Genesis 12:5
Shechem—Genesis 12:6-7
Bethel—Genesis 12:8
Beer-sheba (in the Negev)—Genesis 12:9
Egypt—Genesis 12:10-20
Return from Egypt—Genesis 13:1,3

(You may print references for the return from Egypt in a different color.)
5. Letter title at top of posterboard. Your map will be more attractive if you color the edges of the bodies of water with blue and lightly shade the fertile crescent with green.
6. Cover the front of the board with clear contact plastic.
7. Push a brad through at each of the 6 dots. Attach the red yarn to the brad at Ur.

How to use:

You may use this game as a review after a Sunday School unit on Abraham, or in a Children's Church unit, "How well do you know your Bible geography?"

Have pupils look up the Bible reference and check their maps to locate the geographical area. Choose one pupil to print the name of the place on the map with a water soluble felt-tip pen and wind the yarn around the appropriate brad. (Clear contact plastic over your map allows you to wipe lettering off so that you can use the game again. Pupils may continue until entire journey is completed—all the way to Egypt and back to Bethel. In between each part of the map activity you can emphasize Abraham's faith in obeying God and believing His promise to bless him and give him the land.

Bed Sheet Bible Map

Aims: Juniors

To acquaint pupils with the topography of the land in which Jesus lived.

To help pupils identify biblical sites and tell one event that occurred there.

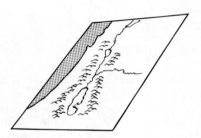

Materials:
1 flat twin bed sheet (green, if possible)
Blue crayon or liquid embroidery pen. (Color will remain when sheet is washed.)
Ball point pen, fiber-tip pen, scissors, ruler
Construction paper: red, green, tan
overhead projector, 8″ x 11″ clear plastic acetate sheet
Atlas of the Bible Lands, Bible handbook

Procedure:
1. Place clear plastic sheet on a Bible map. Trace outline of coastline, Sea of Galilee, Jordan River, and Dead Sea.
2. Hang sheet on wall and project map on it. With ball point pen, lightly draw lines on the sheet.
3. Take down sheet and draw over lines with blue crayon or liquid embroidery pen. (Do *not* use a fiber-tip pen for this, as color will bleed and not remain clear.)
4. Print name of Bible cities on small slips of red construction paper, choosing places mentioned in recent lessons.

5. Cut out Bible mountains from green or tan construction paper. Consult the Bible atlas and cut paper according to the height of the mountains, allowing about 1″ per 1,000 feet. (For example, Mount Hermon is approximately 9,000 feet high. Fold a strip of construction paper so it stands 9″ high when folded.) Cut the paper into a mountain shape. Label the mountain.

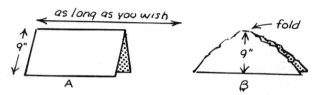

6. Print a Bible reference on the back of city cards and on the inside fold of mountains for pupils to look up. Choose references from stories you have studied recently, or look in a Bible handbook for appropriate references.

Optional procedure for a more realistic map:
If you want your map to be more realistic, make bodies of water from blue fabric and place on the map. Fold towels or pillow cases and lay *under* the sheet on both sides of the Jordan Valley, so that pupils can see the Jordan rift. Fold towels about 1″ high on each side of the Jordan Valley. Then gradually let the towels slope down to the coastline. Towels should stay 1″ high on east side of valley, as there is a flat high plateau on that side.

How to use:
Ask pupils to remove their shoes, as they will be walking on the map. Distribute a city label or mountain to each pupil. Have him identify his place by looking at the Bible atlas map. Then have him look up the Scripture reference. He may then place his card or mountain on the proper place on the sheet and be ready to tell one event that happened there.

floor   sheet   towels   Jordan Valley

Mediterranean Sea

Cross-section view

23

Bible Story Puzzle Tablet

Aims:

To recall past Bible stories.
To introduce Bible stories to children who have been absent from Sunday School.

a.
cut picture

This is the way your pictures should look

b.
divider page

c.
duplicate page

Bible Story Puzzle Tablet

d.
cover

r
e
c
a
l
l

Materials:

Posterboard, snap rings, bright-colored contact plastic
Fiber-tip pen, rubber cement, construction paper, hole punch
2 sets of Bible pictures from recent lessons

Procedure:

1. Glue pictures on construction-paper pages.
2. Cut one copy of each picture into three equal sections. (Avoid cutting through faces.)
3. Punch holes in each section of cut pictures and also in duplicate pictures (sketches a and c).
4. Make a divider page to go between the puzzle and answer sections of the tablet (sketch b).
5. For tablet covers, cut 2 pieces of posterboard an inch larger than picture pages. Cover with colored contact plastic. Punch holes. On the front cover print, "Bible Story Puzzle Tablet."
6. Arrange the tablet in this order:
   front cover
   puzzle section (cut pictures that are scrambled)
   divider page
   answer section (complete pictures)
   back cover
   Insert 3 rings.

How to use:

Let children review recent stories by matching up pictures and telling the stories.

Or take puzzle tablet to a child who has been absent. Go through the pictures in the back first, explaining that these pictures were of the stories he missed when he was absent. Then let the child try to match pictures in the front section.

Picture Puzzle

Pre-primaries
Young Primaries

Aim:
To put together a Bible picture and retell the story.

Materials:
Large Bible teaching picture, posterboard
Rubber cement, scissors, clear plastic contact

Procedure:
1. Glue large picture to posterboard.
2. Cover with clear plastic contact for durability.
3. Cut picture into large pieces. (Do not cut through faces.)

How to use:
Puzzle may be used in a variety of situations: at home, in Sunday School presession or at the end of a lesson. Have children put puzzle together. Ask them if they remember the Bible story from the picture. Have them retell it as much as possible. As they work on the puzzle, guide the conversation so that you can apply the truth of this Bible story to their lives.

Then and Now

Aim:
To discover how Jesus lived as a boy in comparison to how we live today.

"now"

"then"

r
e
c
a
l
l

r
e
i
n
f
o
r
c
e

Materials:
Pictures from your file and from the Bible Picture Dictionary Sets (see p. 48).
Rubber cement, orange and green construction paper or poster-board, scissors

Procedure:
1. Cut construction paper or posterboard to uniform size for pictures. Mount pictures of the following Bible-time items on orange background:
   dishes
   sundial   couch and table   bed
   oil lamp   Palestinian house   goat-skin bag
2. Glue the modern counterpart for each Bible-time item on green posterboard. Be certain there is one modern picture for every Bible-time picture.

How to use:
Let pupils match Bible-time pictures to modern pictures. Then ask if they can recall Bible stories in which the Bible-time items were used.

Wax Paper Box Puzzle

Pre-primaries
Young Primaries

Aim:
To recall and reinforce Bible stories.

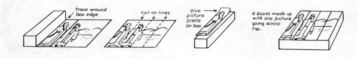

r
e
c
a
l
l

r
e
i
n
f
o
r
c
e

Materials:
4 empty wax paper boxes, 4 Bible teaching pictures 11" x 14"
Glue, scissors, construction paper, clear contact plastic

Procedure:
1. Remove or cover cutting edge from wax paper boxes.
2. Using a box as a measure, divide each picture into 4 pieces the size of the 4 sides of the box. Do this by laying box on the picture and drawing a line along its edge. Repeat twice (sketch a).
3. Cut picture into 4 strips (sketch b).
4. Glue a piece of each picture on each box (sketch c). Important: Do one picture at a time. Each box should have one piece of each picture glued to it.
5. Glue construction paper on box ends.
6. Cover all sides of boxes with clear plastic for protection.

How to use:
Use in presession in Sunday School or as a review activity after Children's Church. Have pupils put together a picture of a Bible story they have had. Then let them explain as much as they can about the picture. Ask pupils to turn the boxes on their sides and try to put together another picture.

—MARION PARKER, VAN NUYS, CALIF.

Egg Carton Shake

Aims: Primaries
To identify individuals and the part they had in Bible stories.
To recall Bible stories of recent units.

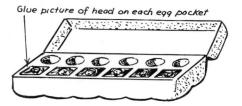

Glue picture of head on each egg pocket

Materials:
Egg carton, Bible story pictures
Scissors, glue, button

Procedure:
1. Cut out small heads of Bible characters from Bible story pictures.
2. Glue one head to the inside of each cup of the egg carton.

How to use:
Put button in egg carton. Close lid. Have a pupil shake carton and lift lid. He should identify the person on which the button landed. If possible, have him tell the Bible story about that person. To make recall and reinforcement more effective, have teaching pictures handy that correspond with Bible characters inside the carton.

—DIANNE ROUTT, FULLERTON, CALIF.

29

Felt Memory Verses

Older Primaries
Young Juniors

Aim:
To help pupils memorize Scripture verses.

r
e
c
a
l
l

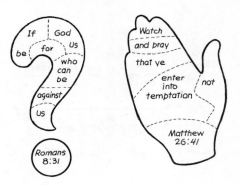

Materials:
Paper and pencil, pieces of felt or flannel
Scissors, fiber-tip pen

Procedure:
1. Sketch a pattern for a Bible memory verse in a shape that helps illustrate the meaning of the verse. Draw lines to indicate separate pieces of a puzzle.
2. With fiber-tip pen draw the pattern on felt or flannel and hand-letter the verse neatly.
3. Cut out outline and then cut separate pieces of puzzle.

How to use:
Put complete verse on the flannel-board and teach the verse. Once children know what the whole verse means, use the process of elimination to teach the words, removing one piece at a time. When you feel the verse has been learned, scramble pieces on the flannel-board and have pupils try to put the verse together in a limited time.

Match-n-Tell

Aims:
To identify Bible-time objects.
To match Bible objects to related Bible stories.
To stimulate pupils to apply Bible truths to their lives today.

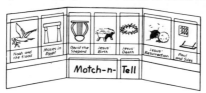

Materials:
Plastic Pocket Tri-Folder (see pp. 6-7).
Bible Picture Dictionary Sets (see p. 48).
Construction paper, scissors, rubber cement, fiber-tip pens.

Procedure:
1. Cut out and mount pictures to fit upper-level pockets of Tri-Folder:
   harp   dove   crown of thorns   manger
   prison   tomb   lintel
2. Hand-letter game title on construction paper to fit lower-level pockets.
3. Hand-letter Bible story titles on construction paper cards to fit middle-level pockets:

Noah and the Flood	Jesus' Death
Moses in Egypt	Jesus' Resurrection
David the Shepherd	Paul and Silas
Jesus' Birth	

How to use:
Insert Bible story titles into middle-level pockets of Tri-Folder. Display pictures on a table. Ask a pupil to insert the picture into top-level pocket that matches one of the Bible story titles. Let him explain something about the object. Guide the conver-

r
e
c
a
l
l

r
e
s
p
o
n
s
e

sation so that he can give life application in his own words. The following questions may help you.

Noah—What kind of promise did God give Noah? (A rainbow to show that He would never flood the earth again.) What kind of promises does God give us today?

Moses—Who does God give us today as our spiritual leader? (Our pastor.) How does our leader help us? (He teaches us God's Word, loves us, and shows us how to serve God.)

David—Who played the harp? Whom did he sing about when he played the harp? (He praised God.) How can we praise God today?

Jesus' Birth—Jesus was God's greatest Gift to us. What gifts can we give to Jesus?

Jesus' Death—Why did Jesus die? (Because He loves us so much that He took the punishment we deserve for our sins.) How can we thank Him for this?

Jesus' Resurrection—What does Jesus promise will happen to Christians after they die?

Paul and Silas—Were Paul and Silas afraid in prison? Who took care of them? Can you think of some ways God takes care of us today?

"Who Am I?" Guessing Game

Aim:
To reinforce the basic concept of God's creation.

Materials:
A paper grocery sack for each player
Picture for each sack of a bird, flower, fruit, animal, baby,
fiber-tip pen, scissors, glue, clear contact plastic, masking tape

Procedure:
1. Cut up on sides of paper sacks so they will fit over shoulders of children. Cut holes for eyes.
2. Color around eye holes and print caption, "God made me."
3. Glue a picture on the front bottom half of each sack.
4. Cover front of sack with clear contact plastic and reinforce raw edges of sack with masking tape.
6. Optional: puncture sides of sacks with fork for air holes.

How to use:
The object of this game is to have the player guess the picture on the front of his sack. Show sacks to children and let them identify the pictures on each. This will help familiarize them with the pictures so that they will be able to guess who they are later.

Read the words at the top of the sacks. Explain that they are going to play a game and that the person who wears the sack has to guess what he is by asking questions which other children will answer with a "yes" or "no." Before asking each question the player should say, "God made me."

Be the first player yourself so that children can follow the game confidently. Have someone put a sack over your head. Say, "God made me—am I something to eat?" Children may answer only "yes" or "no." When you guess correctly what you are, remove the sack and choose a child to be the next player. Be sure he does not see the picture on the front of his sack as you put it on.

—Carolyn Shipway, Garden Grove, Calif.

Does It Fit?

Aim:
To help pupils recognize that Jesus is the Son of God.

Materials:
Posterboard, picture of Jesus
Scissors, fiber-tip pen, glue

Procedure:
1. Cut a half sheet of posterboard into a shape similar to sketch a. This is the main puzzle piece. Glue a picture of Jesus near the bottom and letter the caption.
2. Prepare the matching section to fit into the main piece and letter on it, "the Christ, the Son of God."
3. Prepare 5 other pieces that do *not* fit the main piece. Print one of the following on each:
   a wonderful Lord."   a good man."
   a master teacher."   a miracle worker."
   a healer."

How to use:
Refer pupils to the account of Peter's confession (Matt. 16:13-18). Show question part of the puzzle and the 5 incorrect answer pieces. Pupils may then try to "match" each with the main piece. This gives you opportunity to clarify why each will not fit. Then ask pupils who Peter said Jesus was. Show the correct matching piece and let a pupil fit it into the main piece to reinforce the truth that there is only one correct answer.

This game may be adapted to various lessons to reinforce correct answers.

—Charlotte Iaquinta, Santa Ana, Calif.

"We Love Jesus" Pocket Game

Aim:
                                                Pre-primaries
To give children opportunity to show ways they can express their love for Jesus.

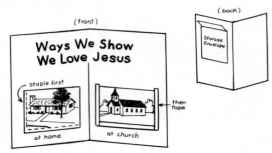

Materials:
Posterboard, pictures from your files
Light-colored construction paper or manila tag
Stapler, tape, fiber-tip pen, glue,
clear contact plastic, large kraft or mailing envelope.

Procedure:
1. On a piece of construction paper or manila tag glue a picture of a church. On another glue a picture of a house.
2. Fold posterboard in half for ease in standing and storage.
3. Place mounted pictures of the church and house on either side of the board and staple sides and bottoms to form pockets. Reinforce pockets by taping over staples.
4. Hand-letter captions across the top of the board and under each pocket.
5. Mount pictures on construction paper, trimming so they will fit in pockets. Choose as subjects children helping parents, sharing, playing happily with others, cleaning up at Sunday School, singing, etc.
6. *Optional:* Cover posterboard with clear plastic contact for protection. If you do this, slit the plastic at the top of each pocket so that pictures can be inserted.

7. Glue a large envelope on the back of the game for storing pictures.

Optional: If you prefer to use the Plastic Pocket Tri-Folder (see pp. 6-7), simply insert title in middle plastic pocket. Insert the pictures of the home and church opposite each other in upper plastic pockets and the appropriate captions in lower pockets. Children may insert mounted pictures behind the captions.

How to use:

Remind children that we can show our love for Jesus in many ways everywhere we go, but in this game you will be thinking of two important places: home and church. Give a child a picture and let him describe it. Ask him to tell how the child pictured is showing he loves Jesus. Then have your pupil put the picture into the pocket he feels it fits. When all the pictures have been used, pupils may tell of other ways they can show their love for Jesus in the coming week.

Making Choices

Aim:
To choose actions that please God.

Materials:
Posterboard, light-colored construction paper or manila tag
Stapler, tape, fiber-tip pen
Clear contact plastic, large kraft or mailing envelope

Procedure:
Follow directions for "We Love Jesus" Pocket Game (pp. 36-37), substituting art on pockets and word cards for pictures to be inserted in pockets.

Label word cards:

help others	good work	take turns
be neat	smile	sing
pray	be friendly	obey
forgive	share	listen to Bible stories
quarrel	steal	fuss
pout	hit	be unkind
be selfish	break a promise	be angry
throw clothes on floor	want to be first always	

You may want to add to the list.

Optional: This game may be adapted for use with the Plastic Tri-Folder by following directions on pages 6-7.

How to use:
May be used at home, in Sunday School, or Children's Church. Mix word cards in a pile. Ask a pupil to take the one on top and choose which pocket it matches. Ask him to tell why it belongs there. If he chooses a "good" item, ask him to tell of a specific time he can do this.

—MARION PARKER, VAN NUYS, CALIF.

Me? A Scaredy-Cat?

Aims: **Older Primaries**

To provide opportunities for pupils to share how they would be loyal to Jesus in front of their friends.

To discuss specific situations in which they can trust Jesus for help when they have problems.

Sketch lower part of face on bottom of sack, as well as side.

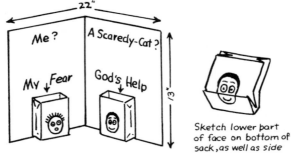

Sketch lower part of face on bottom of sack, as well as side

Materials:

Posterboard; 2 small grocery sacks, about 5″ width

Glue; fiber-tip pen; scissors

Multi-colored 3″ x 5″ cards or construction paper cut to fit size of sacks.

Procedure:

1. Cut posterboard to 22″ x 13″; fold in center.
2. Print captions as shown in sketch.
3. Cut sacks to 6″ height.
4. Draw a scared face on one sack and a happy face on the other. Do this with bottom of sack facing you. Draw the lower part of each face again so that when the sacks are open the full face can still be seen.
5. Glue sacks on posterboard so that when the folder stands open sacks will be level with bottom of posterboard.
6. Print each problem on a separate card, using a different color for each problem. Print the corresponding Bible verse on a card of matching color.

response

39

How to use:
Have a pupil draw a card from the "My Fear" sack and read it aloud to the class. Ask him to tell what he would do in the situation. Then have him find the card with the matching color in the "God's Help" sack. He may read the verse to discover God's answer. Ask him to explain what the verse means and what God would want him to do in the problem situation. Pupils may think of other situations in which they can trust God for their fears.

Questions for "My Fear" sack:	**Bible verse for "God's Help" sack:**
What if I shared my lunch with someone nobody else liked?	Psalm 41:1
What if someone called me "chicken" because I wouldn't hit back?	Matthew 5:9
What if my friend saw me run my skateboard over a neighbor's flowers by accident?	Romans 12:17b
What if my friend dared me to pick up a candy bar in the supermarket?	Hebrews 2:18
What if I invited a neighbor to Sunday School and he called me "stupid"?	Mark 5:19; Hebrews 13:6

Promise Pocket

Aims:
To stimulate pupils to learn promises from God's Word.
To use the Promise Pocket for encouragement in daily life.

Materials:
12" x 18" construction paper, crayons or fiber-tip pens, pencils, stapler, ruler, hole punch
Bibles, 3" x 5" cards
Sample promise pocket for pupils to copy

Procedure:
1. Fold a piece of 12" x 18" construction paper 4½" up from the bottom. Staple sides to make a pocket.
2. Fold down from top 6½". Punch a hole 1" from the top.
3. On inside flap print, "God always keeps His Word." On outside print, "My Pocket of Promises."
4. On the inside, just below the fold line, print, "God promises to help me when . . .
5. On the pocket itself, draw lines to make 6 sections. Hand letter words, as shown in sketch.

How to use:
On the first Sunday of a unit which stresses God's promises, have each pupil make his Promise Pocket. If time allows, he may print the first verse on a 3" x 5" card. He should also put the code number on the top left corner of the card that corresponds to the number on the front of the Pocket.

r
e
s
p
o
n
s
e

41

Each Sunday he may print one or two promises on a 3″ x 5″ card and place it in the pocket. On the last Sunday of the unit, he may take it home and hang it in his room. Whenever he needs the Lord's help, he can look at the front of the pocket and select the box that fits how he feels. Then he may remove the promise that corresponds to the number on the pocket front. Encourage him to use this often and to memorize the verses.

1. am sad—Hebrews 13:5b
2. am afraid—Isaiah 41:13
3. get angry—Matthew 5:9
4. feel alone—Matthew 28:20
5. am tempted to do wrong—James 1:12
6. am worried—1 Peter 5:7

Missionaries Now

Aim: **Older Primaries**

To have pupils draw and explain ways they can be missionaries now.

Materials:

Plastic Pocket Tri-Folder (see pp. 6-7)
Construction paper; crayons or fiber-tip pens; scissors

Procedure:

1. Hand letter the game title on construction paper cards to fit the lower level of the Tri-Folder.
2. Print the following Bible references on construction paper cards to fit the middle-level pockets:

Mark 5:19	2 Corinthians 9:7b
Colossians 3:20	Ephesians 6:18
1 Timothy 6:18	Ephesians 4:32
Isaiah 6:8	

How to use:

Use as an expressional activity after a missionary story in Sunday School or in a missionary education unit for Children's Church.

Insert game title, "Missionaries Now," in lower-level pocket and the Bible reference cards in the middle-level pockets. Give each pupil a piece of construction paper. Let him choose one of the Bible references and look up the verse. (Be sure all ref-

r
e
s
p
o
n
s
e

erences are used.) He may draw in stick figures one way he can be a missionary now, as shown in his verse.

Examples:

Mark 5:19—tell what God has done for you

Colossians 3:20—obey your parents

1 Timothy 6:18—share what you have

Isaiah 6:8—witness

2 Corinthians 9:7b—be a cheerful giver

Ephesians 6:18—pray

Ephesians 4:32—be kind

When the drawings are completed, have each pupil insert his picture in the pocket directly above the Bible reference. He should be ready to explain: what the verse shows about being a missionary now and what his picture shows he can do to obey the verse. If you have more pupils than pockets, simply insert the next pupil's picture on top of the previous one.

Facing My Feelings

Aims:

To provide opportunity for pupils to identify their feelings honestly.

To lead them in discovering how God can help them in everyday situations.

To help them realize that God wants them to thank Him for their happy times and to ask His help with problems.

Materials:
Posterboard; construction paper
2 pieces of clear acetate plastic 4 " x 6½ "
11 3 " x 5 " cards; fiber-tip pen
Mystic or cloth tape; masking tape; Scotch tape

Procedure:
1. Cut 2 pieces of clear acetate plastic 4 " x 6½ "
2. Place plastic pieces on posterboard so that top of each piece is about 12 " from bottom of posterboard. (Leave room for a fold in middle of posterboard.) Tape sides and bottom of plastic to form pockets.
3. Cut an egg-shaped pattern approximately 5 " x 6 ", slightly flat on bottom and narrowing at top. Use this pattern to make 8 faces, choosing a different color of construction paper for each face. Follow sketches to draw appropriate facial expressions. Label faces on back.

r
e
s
p
o
n
s
e

45

4. Attach eight 5″ strips of paper to posterboard with masking tape, following sketch for placement.
5. Add hand-lettered labels and Bible references for the pocket strips and caption to top of board.
6. Above the plastic pocket on right side of board print, "What would my feelings be if. . . ."
7. Hand-letter "feeling" cards as listed below and place in this pocket.
8. Glue a large envelope on back for storing faces and cards when game is not in use.

How to use:
Place faces in appropriate pocket strips. Let a pupil read a "feeling" card and choose a face that matches his response. He may place the face in the plastic pocket on the left side of the board and tell how he would feel in that situation. Either he or the group may then look up the appropriate Scripture to discover how God can help him with his feelings.

Follow this procedure until all "feeling" cards have been used.

Remind pupils that God wants us to tell Him honestly both our sad feelings and our happy, thankful feelings. Ask pupils to think of other times they may feel one of the ways shown on the board. A recent translation or paraphrase may be helpful.

"Feeling cards:
What would my feelings be like if . . .
. . . someone squeezed in ahead of me at lunch line at school?
. . . someone stole my bike?
. . . I wanted a part in the school play, but the teacher chose someone else?
. . . my mom surprised me with my favorite dessert when I got home from school?
. . . my friend invited me to a party, but I had to clean my room instead?
. . . there were an earthquake (or tornado) and our house started to shake?
. . . my school class had an outing, but I got sick and couldn't go?
. . . the only way I could join my friend's secret club would be to share my math answers?
. . . my pet died?
. . . everyone in class got a good grade on a test, except me?

. . . I got separated from my family on a camping-hiking trip?

. . . my dad got real sick, and then the doctor said he was going to be OK?

References to print above pocket strips:

Sad: John 14:1; 1 Peter 5:7

Thankful: 1 Thessalonians 5:18

Tempted: Hebrews 2:18

Mad: Matthew 5:9; Romans 12:18

Disappointed: Romans 8:28

Lonely: Hebrews 13:5b

Scared: Psalm 91:11, 15; Genesis 28:15a

Happy: Proverbs 15:13a

Tips on Creating
Your Own Bible Games

Ask yourself:

WHO will be playing the game?

Be sure it fits the ability level and interests of the children who will be playing.

WHY should the children play it? What is your purpose? Is it research, recall, reinforcement, or response?

HOW should the game be played?

As you answer this question you will think through the game step by step and sketch a diagram.

WHAT materials should be used?

Gather all the needed materials *before* you begin making the game.

HOW will you introduce the game?

List your procedure in writing so that you can acquaint children with the rules *before* they begin to play.

Supply Checklist

Tools

Most of the games in this manual can be made with a few simple tools.

You'll need: fiber-tip pens, both wide and narrow tipped, reliable ruler and yardstick, scissors, glue, rubber cement, stapler, paper punch

Art supplies

Visit art and office supply and hardware stores to acquaint yourself with the kinds of supplies that are available and the best prices. You'll need: posterboard (22″ x 28″) and construction paper (9″ x 12″ and 12″ x 18″) in a variety of colors; manila tag, kraft or mailing envelopes for storing game parts, Mystic or cloth covered tape, clear contact plastic for laminating game surfaces

Pictures and maps

To get the most teaching value from your games you will need pictures and maps that have been carefully researched for accuracy. Start to build a file of pictures from extra take-home papers, used teaching aids and pupil manuals.

You will also find it worthwhile to invest in Bible Picture Dictionary Sets, which are available from your local Christian bookstore or Scripture Press, Box 1825, Wheaton, Ill. 60187. Many of the games in this manual use pictures from these sets. You will need one complete set to cut apart for the games and a duplicate set to make up into a loose-leaf dictionary for pupils to use in checking their answers.

Order *one* Bible Picture Dictionary Index—16 tabbed 9″ x 11″ alphabetical dividers, 3-hole punched, No. 7-3750, $1.00.

Order *two* of the following picture sets (one for the dictionary and the other for use in the games), only 60¢ each:

Bible Picture Dictionary

Set No. 1—7-3754	Set No. 4—7-3777	Set No. 6—7-3779
Set No. 2—7-3775	Set No. 5—7-3778	Set No. 7—7-3755
Set No. 3—7-3776		

For map games you will need a Bible atlas. Order *Atlas of the Bible Lands,* No. 7-3741, $1.50.

A Bible handbook is a gold mine of background information usable in games. We recommend *Eerdman's Handbook to the Bible,* No. 8-8938, $12.95.

NOTE: Prices subject to change.